Sparkling stories

Christmas tales to read aloud!

**Brian Ogden,
Marjory Francis,
Robert Harrison
and others!**

Copyright © Gillian Ellis, Marjory Francis, Robert Harrison, Brian Ogden,
Isla Plumtree and Michael Wells 2004
First published 2004
ISBN 1 85999 796 1

Scripture Union, 207–209 Queensway, Bletchley, Milton Keynes, MK2 2EB, England
Email: info@scriptureunion.org.uk
Website: www.scriptureunion.org.uk

Scripture Union Australia, Locked Bag 2, Central Coast Business Centre, NSW 2252
Website: www.scriptureunion.org.au

Scripture Union USA, PO Box 987, Valley Forge, PA 19482
Website: www.scriptureunion.org

The right of Gillian Ellis, Marjory Francis, Robert Harrison, Brian Ogden, Isla Plumtree and
Michael Wells to be identified as authors of this work has been asserted by them in accordance
with the Copyright, Designs and Patents Act 1988.

Scripture quotations are from the Contemporary English Version published by HarperCollins
Publishers, Copyright © 1991, 1992, 1995 American Bible Society.

'Maximus Mouse's unexpected visitors' appeared previously as 'Unexpected visitors: Christmas'
in Maximus and the Computer Mouse, published by Scripture Union, 1997.

British Library Cataloguing-in-Publication Data.
A catalogue record of this book is available from the British Library.

Printed and bound in Great Britain by Creative Print and Design (Wales) Ebbw Vale.

Cover design: fourninezero design

Scripture Union is an international Christian charity working with churches in more than
130 countries, providing resources to bring the good news about Jesus Christ to children, young
people and families and to encourage them to develop spiritually through the Bible and prayer.

As well as our network of volunteers, staff and associates who run holidays, church-based
events and school Christian groups, we produce a wide range of publications and support those
who use our resources through training programmes.

Contents

Most of these Sparkling Stories can be enjoyed at any time over the Christmas period. But to help you to make your choice, we've suggested which stories may be more suitable for various times in the festive season.

Stories set in the run-up to Christmas

Stories for Christmas Eve or Christmas Day

Stories for after Christmas

The mince pie tooth

(Reading time: 10 minutes)

Storytelling tip: if you're able to show Christmas cards with shepherds on, this would add to the story. You could set up a small display of these cards in the place where you'll be telling the story.

It was the mince pie that did it. One bite into Granny's golden pastry and the tooth jumped out of Jake's mouth and dropped with a 'clink' onto the plate. Jake looked at it in astonishment. He had known his tooth was wobbly but he hadn't expected it to come out so soon.

'That's done it,' said Lydia. 'You won't be able to be in the Christmas play now. They won't want a shepherd with an ugly face.'

'I will thtill be a thepherd,' insisted Jake.

'Huh, you can't even talk properly now,' said Lydia.

'Yeth I can!' shouted Jake.

'Lydia,' warned Dad, 'don't tease. You know it's perfectly normal for front teeth to fall out when you're about 6. Yours did.' Dad called Jake over.

'Come here, old man. Let's have a look at that gap. Wow! I reckon Miss Thompson will put you on the front row of the shepherds with that smile!'

Nobody had noticed Barney licking his lips and wagging his

tail, but Lydia thought she'd better make up for being nasty to Jake, so she picked up the empty plate from the floor where it had fallen, and took it out to the kitchen. She dusted the crumbs into the bin and put the plate in the sink.

'Thank you, darling,' said Mum.

'Jake's tooth's come out,' remarked Lydia.

'Has it?' said Mum. 'Jake! Let's see your tooth.'

'It's here, Mum,' said Jake, running into the kitchen and grinning widely. 'I bit a mince pie and it came out.'

'I can see the gap,' smiled Mum, 'but where's the tooth?'

'Oh, I forgot. It fell on the plate.' Jake ran back to the sitting room and looked round, while Mum and Lydia looked at each other in dismay.

'Oh dear,' said Mum quietly. 'It must have gone down the plughole.'

Dad gulped. He found the quiet evening he'd been looking forward to was changing into one which involved unscrewing pipes, taking things to pieces and, if he wasn't careful, a flood in the kitchen before he got them together again.

'Are you sure you need this tooth?' asked Dad.

'Yes,' insisted Jake. 'I want to show it to Miss Thompson.'

'Well, I suppose it's a good opportunity to clean this sink pipe out properly,' said Dad, bravely poking a finger into some rather nasty looking gunge he'd found, 'but there's no sign of your tooth, Jake. It was probably washed away.'

Jake's eyes began to fill with tears. He discovered he was really missing his tooth, and he did want to show it to Miss Thompson.

Suddenly Lydia said, 'Wait a minute. I put the crumbs from the plate into the bin. Perhaps Jake's tooth fell in there and not down the sink.'

Everyone looked at everyone else. No one wanted to look in the bin! Eventually Mum took a deep breath and rolled up her sleeves. It was unbelievable what she tipped out of the bin onto a plastic bag – sticky apple cores, slimy banana skins, quickly-on-the-way-to-being-mouldy carrot and potato peelings, all mixed up with messy baked bean tins and the screwed-up (and very smelly) paper that had been wrapped round yesterday's fish and chips. As well as these there were some chewed-looking chicken bones (Barney hovered round hopefully, but Mum shooed him away), a few old letters, and some very dead chrysanthemums.

'Is it there? Is it there?' asked Jake, bouncing up and down beside Mum. Mum gingerly lifted up the last slimy banana skin. No tooth was lurking underneath. Jake's face fell. He looked as if he was about to cry.

Lydia was staring at all the rubbish with a thinking look on her face.

'Did you eat the mince pie, Jake?' she asked.

'No, I only bit it,' he said.

'Then where is it,' asked Lydia, 'if it's not in the bin?'

'Barney!' Everyone's eyes turned to look accusingly at the dog, who was looking as if he hadn't eaten anything for hours.

'If Barney ate the mince pie, perhaps he swallowed the tooth as well,' said Lydia.

Jake burst into tears. 'Barney's eaten my tooth! He's a horrible dog!' he wailed. 'I wanted to take my tooth to school to show Miss Thompson and Barney's eaten it.'

Mum gave Jake a big cuddle. 'Oh darling, what a thing to happen! Let's hope Barney doesn't get tummy ache if he has swallowed it.'

Jake began to howl. He didn't care if Barney had tummy ache. It would serve him right! Everything had gone wrong. He knew he wouldn't enjoy being in the Christmas play without his tooth. It wasn't fair! He sobbed for a long time.

Nothing anyone said seemed to help, so Mum just sat with

him on her lap, while Dad and Lydia went into the kitchen to scoop the mess back into the rubbish bin. Lydia turned on the tap to wash her chicken-boney and baked-beany hands, but unfortunately Dad hadn't fixed the pipe under the sink yet. The water ran straight out on the kitchen floor.

'I hope that dog's not expecting a Christmas present from me,' said Dad, 'because at the moment I don't feel like giving him one!'

By the time the kitchen was all clean again, Jake had calmed down a bit. Mum asked him to help her arrange the Christmas cards along the mantelpiece, and they looked at each one carefully as they put it in place.

'They look good,' said Dad, coming in. 'I see you've put all the ones with shepherds at the front.'

'Dad,' asked Jake, 'did the real shepherds have teeth?'

'Yes, I'm sure they did,' smiled Dad. 'Well, some of the old ones didn't perhaps. People weren't able to look after their teeth in those days as well as we can, and sometimes when they got old their teeth would fall out.'

Jake frowned. He didn't want to look like an old shepherd.

'What about Jesus? Did he have teeth?'

'He wouldn't have when he was a baby,' said Dad. 'Babies aren't usually born with teeth. But then he would have grown some little ones like you and when he was about 6 they would have fallen out, just like yours did.'

'Bedtime, I think,' said Mum, hastily changing the subject. 'Can't have you all dozy at the Christmas play tomorrow.'

'Come on, old man,' said Dad. 'I'll take you up and read you a story. Let's put your slippers on.'

Jake sleepily pulled on his rabbit slippers. 'Ouch, there's a stone in this one,' he said. Mum felt inside – and brought out a little pearly tooth!

Jake was tucked up cosily in bed. Everything was all right now. The tooth, which Barney must have knocked into the slipper when he ate the mince pie, was safely in an envelope in his school bag, ready for him to show Miss Thompson. How pleased she would be to see it! Then he thought of his shepherd costume, hanging on the string across the classroom with all the others, waiting for him to dress up for the Christmas play. He imagined himself standing on the stage with all the other shepherds and singing the song about baby Jesus. Everyone would see the gap where his tooth had been, but perhaps he didn't care.

Jake remembered about Jesus being a real little boy like him and having teeth that fell out, and he smiled.

'Dad', he said, 'it was the mince pie that made my tooth come out. I wonder if Jesus ate a mince pie.'

Jake giggled at the thought. Dad grinned too, and then they both laughed for a long time. At last Jake snuggled contentedly down under the duvet.

'Thank you, Jesus, for teeth, and shepherds – and for mince pies,' said Jake. 'Goodnight, Dad.'

Marjory Francis

When Marjory was a teacher, one of her favourite parts of the day was storytime. She still enjoys telling and listening to stories, and hopes you do too.

Prayer idea:

It's Christmas! Thank you, God, for all the things that make this time of year special. Thank you for your Son, Jesus. Amen.

It's my birthday, too!
The Diary of Sam, aged nearly 9

(Reading time: 15 minutes)

Monday, 15th December

Yes! Last week of school before Christmas. We don't have many normal lessons before Christmas – it's great! Our Assembly was longer than ever today – we practised all the carols for the nativity play at least twenty times!

I had a Christmas card from Lauren in Class Four. I haven't done her one. Gareth said, 'She likes you, Sam.' I felt my face get hot. He just laughed.

Tuesday, 16th December

Opened my Advent calendar as normal this morning. Then Mum called me from upstairs. Went back to the calendar and Dad had got to the chocolate first! Huh!

Another rehearsal for the nativity play this afternoon. It was going quite well until George in Year One fell off the stage. It's the third year running I've been a shepherd. Why can't I be a wise man? All right, don't answer that!

I had a card from Sophie in our class. Gareth said, 'She likes you.' I'll have to get her one now.

Wednesday, 17th December

In RE Miss Spence asked which special person has a birthday on Christmas Day. She got really cross when I said, 'Me, Miss!' Everyone laughed – but she didn't. BUT IT IS MY BIRTHDAY ON CHRISTMAS DAY. I was born on December 25th. I can't help it – it just happened that way. I wish it was any day but Christmas Day. I mean, can you think of a worse day to have a birthday?

Mum came to the nativity play. She said I looked just like a shepherd but I shouldn't have scratched my beard so much. All the mums went 'Ah' when Reception came on as angels. Funny angels most of them are – you should see them in the playground!

I had a card from Holly in Class Four today. Gareth said, 'That's three girls that like you!'

Thursday, 18th December

Only a day to go. Mum told us at breakfast about Nanny coming to stay. Then she said, 'Sam, while Nanny's here I want you to share with Jack.' It's always ME that has to move out. Jack's my baby brother – he's 5. Christmas is my birthday and what happens? I have to share Jack's room and wake up and see his United posters everywhere. Why can't he support a decent team?

'Do we have any birthdays this week?' asked Mrs Robinson in Assembly. Everyone with birthdays went out to the front. I thought about it and put up my hand. It was worth a try. Mrs Robinson gave me one of her headteacher looks.

'Yes, Sam?' she said.

'Mine's in the holidays,' I said.

'I expect we'll remember it next term then,' said Mrs Robinson. 'Now, come on everyone. Let's sing our birthday song.'

It's always the same. Ever since I've been in school I've

always missed my birthday song. What a day to have a birthday! I had a card from Jade in our class today.

Friday, 19th December

Last day of school! We all brought in games to play. The teachers put on silly hats from crackers and served Christmas lunch. The best bit was the Christmas pudding, but the worst bit was the SPROUTS! Yuk! Miss Spence gave us all a card. Guess what? She actually remembered it was my birthday on Christmas Day! She wrote, 'I hope you have a very happy birthday', on my card. Phew! Not everyone's forgotten after all. Zoe from Class Three gave me a Christmas card. Thank goodness Gareth didn't see it.

Saturday, 20th December

Mum reminded me that Nanny is arriving on Monday. That means sorting out my bedroom. Well, I like it how it is. Do you have that problem? Adults just don't get why we leave things where they are. So I had a grotty morning sorting it all out. Then we went shopping. It was totally bananas. We couldn't find anywhere to park, the shops were bursting, and everyone seemed in a bad mood. I even heard a Father Christmas shouting. The check-out queues in the supermarket went back for ages.

Dad said, 'I think we'll still be here on Christmas Day.'

I said, 'You mean on my birthday!'

It was six o'clock when we got home and we missed the football results.

Sunday, 21st December

Jack and I got down the Christmas tree and hung up all the cards.

'There's a lot here from girls at school,' said Jack. I ignored him.

Then it was time for the Family Service at church. We had

a quiz today, children against parents, and we won!

After lunch Mum said, 'I'm just going to check your bedroom before Nanny comes.' Well, I thought I'd left it tidy until Mum found some old football socks under the bed. Oops. She came out of the room holding them at arm's length with one hand, and holding her nose with the other...

Monday, 22nd December

I moved my things into Jack's room. Had an argument with him when I tried to stick a City poster over one of his United ones. Then we went to meet Nanny at the station. She had two bags. Jack said, 'Nanny, is that one full of Christmas presents?' Brothers can be really embarrassing. Besides which there should be a birthday present as well as a Christmas present – for me, that is.

Tuesday, 23rd December

Not a lot happened. I don't like writing up my diary in Jack's room. He keeps asking if I'm writing about him. As if...

Wednesday, 24th December

Lots of Christmas cards came, but no birthday cards that I could see. What a day to have a birthday! Mum and Dad went out to do the last minute shopping leaving us to look after Nanny – or was it the other way round? Anyway I took Buster, our dog, for a walk. Guess who I saw? Zoe, from Class Three.

'Sam, did you get my card?' she asked. In front of her mum and dad too. Was I embarrassed!

We hung up our big stockings. I thought Jack would never go to sleep he was so excited. Perhaps he'll sleep later tomorrow?

Thursday, 25th December

The answer is NO! He didn't sleep later; in fact, he woke up at half past five. When Jack's awake so is everyone else in the house, and road and, I should think, town. We took our stockings into Mum and Dad's room. I had some really cool presents – the in-line skates I wanted, a City shirt and a CD.

'Happy Christmas,' said Mum and Dad. You would think THEY might remember it's my birthday and not just Christmas. We'd already been awake three hours before we had breakfast. Then it was time for church.

'I need someone to help me open this parcel,' said the vicar. 'Sam, will you come out please?'

The parcel was really big, and wrapped in snowmen paper. I tore it off. Then there was a second layer with holly and berries. Then there was a third with robins, and a fourth and a fifth. Under the last piece of wrapping paper was a box.

'Go on, Sam,' said the vicar, 'open the box.'

Inside the box was an envelope.

'What do you think is in the envelope?' asked the vicar.

'I suppose it's a Christmas card,' I said.

'Have a look,' he said. I tore open the envelope. It wasn't a Christmas card. It was a birthday card!

'Read the words inside please, Sam.'

'A very happy birthday, Jesus and Sam,' I read.

Then the vicar got everyone in church to shout, 'A very happy birthday, Jesus and Sam!'

'You see,' said the vicar after I sat down, 'when we take off all the wrapping paper what we are left with is Jesus' birthday. That's the most important part of Christmas – that Jesus was born on earth.'

After lunch I had my presents – birthday that is, not

Christmas. And I had a cake with nine candles. It was the best birthday I've ever had. Perhaps having Christmas Day as a birthday isn't so bad – after all, I do share it with Jesus!

Brian Ogden

Brian Ogden has written more than twenty books for Scripture Union, including the ever-popular Maximus Mouse series. For more Christmas fun for younger children from Brian, look out for An Alien for Christmas.

Prayer idea:

Dear God, at Christmas, we celebrate Jesus' birthday. Help us to remember him in all the fun. Amen.

'And they named him Jesus, just as the angel had told Mary when he promised she would have a baby.' Luke 2:21

Not a wise man... AGAIN!

(Reading time: 10 minutes)

Ever since I was three it's been the same. It started when I was in the Nursery. I didn't mind then but five Christmases later I'm fed up with it. The problem is that my name is Casper. And that means one thing – I always end up as a wise man in the nativity play!

You see, some people think that the wise men might have been called Melchior, Balthazzar and Casper. It doesn't say so in the Bible but those are the names that they get called. So because my name is Casper every teacher thinks I want to be a wise man. I DON'T. For five years I have worn a silly dressing gown, put on a hat made from a towel, and carried a pot of pretend frankincense. For five years I've had to kneel down in front of somebody's doll. For five years I've had to sing 'We three kings of Orient are.' I'm surprised I don't sing it in my sleep!

Would things be any different this year? A few weeks ago Mrs King, she's my class teacher, sat us all down on the story mat.

'Mr Beech (he's our headteacher) has asked our class to produce the nativity play this year. It will be a part of the whole Christmas presentation, so other classes will be doing different things.'

'Couldn't we do one of those different things?' I asked hopefully.

'No, Casper,' said Mrs King. 'We are going to act out the

Christmas story. Next week we will go through the story and choose who will play what part.'

A week later we sat on the story mat again. Mrs King had a clipboard in one hand and a pen in the other. I knew what was coming.

'I'm going to remind you about the Christmas story and then we'll begin to choose who is going to play the parts in the nativity play.'

I did a big yawn and got one of Mrs King's teacher looks. The sort that means 'I'm not going to say anything this time but don't let it happen again'.

'The story begins when Mary has a visit from an angel. Mary lived in a town called – can anyone remember?'

'Nazareth,' said Amelia. 'Can I be Mary, please Mrs King?'

'Yes, it was Nazareth,' said Mrs King. 'We'll talk about Mary later, Amelia.'

You see, some people actually like being in the play – but they haven't had the same part for five years!

'The angel told Mary that she was going to have a baby and that the baby would be called Jesus. So we'll need Mary and an angel,' said Mrs King writing down the names. 'Mary was going to marry a man called...?'

'Joseph,' said Toby. 'Can I be Joseph, Mrs King?'

'Later,' said Mrs King, 'now back to the story. One day a Roman soldier came to Nazareth. He told all the people that the Romans were taking a census – that means they wanted to count everyone. All the people had to go to their own home towns. For Joseph and Mary it meant a long journey to...?'

'Bethlehem,' said Jerome. 'Can I be the donkey, Mrs King?'

Everyone laughed. Even Mrs King grinned.

'And what happened in Bethlehem?' she asked, all serious again.

'The hotels were full,' said Emily, 'so Mary and Joseph had to go to a stable.'

'Well done, Emily,' said Mrs King. 'But they weren't hotels like the ones we stay in on holiday. They were very simple inns – not much more than open courtyards. We'll need some innkeepers in our play to tell Joseph and Mary there was no room for them.'

Mrs King carefully wrote down 'innkeepers' on her pad.

'Now, who can tell me what happened to some shepherds on the hills above Bethlehem?'

'They saw angels,' said Ben. 'Can I be a shepherd?'

'We'll see, Ben,' sighed Mrs King. 'Yes, there were angels about on that very special night. They brought a message from God to the shepherds. The angels said that Jesus had been born and they would find him in a manger. We shall need plenty of shepherds and angels.'

Perhaps she's forgotten the wise men, I thought. Perhaps for once I might be something else!

'Then,' said Mrs King, 'some time after the shepherds visited Jesus, some other people came. Who were they?'

'The three wise... OUCH!' said Denzil.

The 'ouch' came because I prodded him. I was lucky – Mrs King didn't see it.

'I think you mean the three wise men, Denzil,' said Mrs King. 'Traditionally we call them Casper, Balthazzar and Melchior.'

'But we don't know what their real names were, do we?' I said rather loudly.

'No, Casper, we don't.' I got another teacher look from Mrs King. 'Now, I've written down all the people who were in the Bible story. I want you to write your name by the part you would like to take. Some of you will be disappointed because we can only have one Mary and one Joseph, but I'll be as fair as I can.'

When Mrs King's list of people in the play came to me I

wrote 'Casper' by 'The Shepherds'. By 'The Wise Men' I wrote, 'NOT CASPER PLEASE' in big writing. I didn't think it would do any good though – teachers always think that with my name, I should be a wise man. We were supposed to be doing maths, but I spent most of the time until break looking at Mrs King. I could see she was beginning to tick or change the names on the play list. I only managed to get one take-away right out of ten. I had to stay in at break and do them all again!

After lunch, Mrs King took out the list of names.

'As I told you this morning, not everyone who wants to play a particular part can have their choice,' she said. 'The problem is we seem to have 14 shepherds and no wise men!'

Oh no! I thought. I'm going to have to be a wise man again. Mrs King looked at me. Here it comes. Why couldn't Mum and Dad have called me William or Henry or John or David or James or Mark – anything but Casper?

'So I have chosen,' said Mrs King, 'Cameron, Emily and Steven to be the three wise men and... er... woman.'

I collected another teacher look when I punched the air and said, 'YES', far too loudly. At last I wasn't going to be a wise man.

'Beth will be Mary and Joseph will be... Joseph,' Mrs King carried on through the list.

So that meant I would be a Roman soldier, an innkeeper or a shepherd.

'Jerome will be a Roman soldier, and Angus, Rory and Mica will be the innkeepers. The shepherds will be Casper...'

I didn't listen any more. I WAS GOING TO BE A SHEPHERD – NOT A WISE MAN. This could be the best Christmas ever!

And it was. For the first time I really listened to what the angel said to the shepherds.

'Don't be afraid! I have good news for you, which will make everyone happy. This very day in King David's home town a

Saviour was born for you.'

And I was a very happy shepherd as I sang 'While shepherds watched their flocks by night' instead of 'We three kings'! But something made it even better. My uncle Matthew is a farmer who lives in the next village. When he heard I was going to be a shepherd (and not a wise man for once!), he let me borrow a real lamb for the Christmas play. That was much more fun than gold, frankincense and myrrh!

Brian Ogden

Prayer idea:

Thank you, God, for the fun things we do at school at Christmas. Thank you for plays, parties and special things to make. Amen.

'That night in the fields near Bethlehem some shepherds were guarding their sheep. All at once an angel came down to them from the Lord, and the brightness of the Lord's glory flashed around them.' Luke 2:8,9

The angel on the tree

(Reading time: 10 minutes)

Storytelling tip: you could use a Christmas tree angel as Angela, and change the description given in the story to match your angel. If you have a crib set, you could use this at the point Mum brings out her crib.

My name is Angel A. I know it's a funny name but in the factory where I was made there were Angel As, Angel Bs and Angel Cs. We were all different from each other. Anyway, I'm Angel A. You can call me Angela. I've got a pretty pink face, big shiny wings and a sparkling white dress. I'm the sort of Christmas decoration that gets thrown away with the tree after Christmas.

A few weeks ago I was bundled into a box and taken with a lot of other angels to a shop. I lay there for ages wondering what was going to happen next.

'Can we have one of those angels?' I heard a girl's voice ask. 'She'd look brilliant on top of our tree.'

'YUK!' said a boy's voice. 'Why can't we have a footballer on the tree?'

'Because,' said an older voice, 'angels are in the Christmas story and footballers are not! Sarah's right, the tree needs an angel.'

I was lifted up, popped in a smaller box, and dropped in a bag. Soon other things were put in the bag – some candles which smelled and some tinsel which didn't. I hoped I was going to have one happy Christmas in a good home with a proper tree.

It seemed ages before the box was opened. Everything had got a bit messed up in the box – my dress was crumpled and my wings were crooked but the humans seemed to like me. I discovered that the girl was called Sarah and the boy was called Mark. The older person was called Mum.

Sarah lifted me up, smoothed down my dress and straightened my wings. In the corner of the room I could see my home for the next few weeks – a real fir tree.

And then it happened.

One minute Sarah was standing on a chair, stretching out towards the tree. She was holding me tight in her hand. The next minute Mark moved the chair and Sarah wobbled.

'STOP IT!' shouted Sarah.

Then – CRASH! I found myself hurtling across the room. Help! Angels are supposed to fly gracefully, not be catapulted! I landed on a huge furry thing which I found out later was called the dog. Sarah was yelling, the dog was barking and I was one terrified angel. Help! Then the dog stopped barking, gave me a good sniff and decided he didn't like me very much. He growled and bared huge white teeth which he was just about to sink in my tummy when Mum came running into the room.

'What on earth is going on?' she said, looking around.

Sarah had fallen on the sofa and bounced off onto the floor. She was crying, the dog was whining and Mark was laughing. The tree had fallen over and there were pine needles all over the carpet. No one seemed bothered about me.

'Right. Mark, you can take Treacle for a walk,' said Mum. 'Sarah, get up and stop making such a fuss. As if I haven't got enough to do without this mess.'

Mum picked up the tree and straightened the branches. She spotted me lying half-under the table.

'Well,' she said, putting me carefully on top of the tree, 'as you can see, you're the only angel in this house! After tea we'll decorate your tree.'

Later Mum, Sarah and Mark hung sparkling tinsel and pretty baubles on the tree's branches. I had a fantastic view from the top of the tree. I could see and hear what everyone was doing and saying. Perhaps I would learn something about Christmas and being an angel.

I was woken up the next morning by the clatter of the letterbox and Treacle barking. Mark rushed to the door. There were lots of envelopes on the doormat.

'Let's open the cards over breakfast,' said Mum, coming downstairs.

Mum and Sarah and Mark sat down to eat. The table was near my tree so I could see what was going on.

'That's a pretty card from Aunty Shirley,' said Mum as she showed it to the children.

I nearly fell off the tree when I saw it. It was a picture of an angel! The angel was talking to a young woman. Sarah looked up at me, then stared at the card.

'That angel doesn't look like ours,' she said. 'Anyway, what's the angel on the card saying to Mary?'

'She's going to have a baby,' said Mark, 'and she's got to call him Jesus. We did it at school last week.'

Sarah looked at the angel on the card again.

'God sent the angel as his messenger,' said Mum. 'He came to tell Mary that she would be the mother of a very special baby, and the baby's name would be Jesus. But Jesus wasn't just Mary's son – he was also the Son of God.'

Mum and the children cleared up and went off shopping. That left me thinking. So Christmas is all about a special baby called Jesus. But what happened when he was born? I hoped there were other angels in the story.

It was much later that day before they all came home again. After they'd had tea Mum put a box on the table. It looked very old. Mark and Sarah sat watching. Mum carefully opened the box and took out some small figures.

'Mum, tell us the story again,' said Sarah.

'This is the crib set that Nanny put out every Christmas when I was your age,' Mum said. 'She gave it to me the year that Mark was born. But there's one figure missing. Can you remember which one from last year?'

'The angel,' said Sarah. 'The one who told the shepherds about Jesus.'

My ears pricked up.

'It's missing because you took it out and played with it,' said Mark, 'and it never got put back in the box.'

Sarah went a bit pink.

I watched as Mum gently lifted out the figures. Sarah started counting on her fingers. 'Mary, Joseph, baby Jesus...' she said.

'...And the shepherds – minus an angel,' added Mark. He stuck his tongue out at Sarah.

'But I know the angel was really important because he came and told the shepherds about the baby,' said Sarah. 'First there was just one angel and then there were lots.'

I was listening hard again.

'The angel told the shepherds that a really special baby had been born in Bethlehem,' said Mum. 'He told them where to find the baby.'

'And the shepherds ran down the hill and found the baby and told Mary and Joseph what the angel had said about him,' finished Sarah.

The family carried on chatting about the crib figures together. But I wasn't listening any more. I could hardly believe it – real angels are messengers from God! One of them told Mary that she was going to have a special baby. Another told the shepherds that the baby had been born. But he wasn't an ordinary baby, he was God's Son. I was thinking about this when something brilliant happened.

'Mum,' said Mark, picking up a shepherd, 'you know how the angel's missing? Well, it isn't any more. We've got one on our tree.'

They all turned and looked at me.

'Please Mum, can we put our angel with the shepherds?' asked Sarah.

'And keep it with the nativity set?' said Mark.

And that's what happened. I didn't get thrown away with the tree after Christmas. And every year after that I stand by the shepherds as part of the nativity set. It was a great start to all my Christmases!

Brian Ogden

Prayer idea:

> Dear God, thank you for the good news the angels gave Mary and the shepherds. Help us to remember Jesus when we look at the angels on our Christmas trees and cards. Amen.

> ' ... *God sent the angel Gabriel to the town of Nazareth in Galilee with a message for a virgin named Mary ... The angel greeted Mary and said, "You are truly blessed! The Lord is with you."'* Luke 1:26-28

The best thing about Christmas

What's the best thing about Christmas?
Is it the tree or the cake?
Is it the crackers or presents?
Is it the biscuits we bake?

Is it the candles or carols?
Is it the lip-smacking smells?
Is it the marzipan icing?
Is it the church and the bells?

Is it the mistletoe berries?
Is it the packets of sweets?
Is it the mince pies and sherry?
Is it the parties and treats?

Is it the holly and ivy?
Is it the snowman and hat?
Is it the crib and the manger?
Is it Dick Whittington's cat?

Is it the ham glazed with honey?
Is it the pantomime dame?
Is it the chocolate money?
Is it the pudding aflame?

Is it the star or the angel?
Is it the cards through the post?
Is it the visit from Grandma?
What is the thing we love most?

Christ's the best thing about Christmas –
Christmas, the time of his birth –
God sent the Saviour at Christmas,
Born to bring love to the earth.

Gillian Ellis

*Gillian Ellis writes mainly for magazines and edits two in-house
quarterlies. She has written five books of resource materials,
also a quarter share in a children's book of short stories.*

The night Jodie went carol-singing

(Reading time: 10 minutes, longer if music is used)

Storytelling tip: you could make this story musical if you have resources available. Sing one or two verses from each carol at the points they're mentioned in the story. An alternative would be to play short clips of the songs from a backing tape. A list of songs featured is given at the end of the story.

The prayer idea given at the end of the story needs song words and music for a popular carol.

Being in the middle of an argument between two big people is no fun when you're 7, Jodie thought. Her mum and sister were arguing, and it was about her.

'But Mum,' Louise was saying, 'I can't stay in and babysit Jodie. It's carol-singing tonight.'

Suddenly Jodie had an idea. 'I know!' she said. 'I could go carol-singing with Louise.'

Louise wasn't sure what Gary, the youth leader, would say about a 7-year-old joining the youth group for an hour. But if it was the only way she'd get to go carol-singing, she'd leave it up to him. After all, it was only until Dad got home.

Gary was happy with the plan. 'Yes, let her come,' he said, smiling at Jodie. 'She can help me collect the money. We won't sing – you know my froggy voice, and I don't suppose Jodie's had time to learn all the words.'

By this time, the youth group had turned up at Jodie's house, number 11 Churchill Square. Last week they had gone round the square, putting notes through letterboxes to tell people they'd be singing tonight, and that they were hoping to collect lots of money to help build a new ward at the local hospital.

The youth group stood together on the grass in the centre of the square and started singing 'Once in royal David's city.' The coloured lanterns they were holding lit up their faces, and their voices sounded lovely in the frosty air. Gary let them sing one verse, then he tugged at Jodie's sleeve.

'Come on,' he said, 'time to start collecting.' They walked down the path of Jodie's next-door neighbour at number 12 and knocked on their first door.

By the time they'd been to about ten houses, people had been really generous and the money tin was beginning to rattle nicely. Jodie was very pleased at the noise it made. As Mr Thomas at number 23 opened the door, she shook the tin very loudly and enthusiastically. Unfortunately, Mr Thomas had come to the door holding his old and rather nervous cat Bitsy, who was startled by the rattling noise. Bitsy scrabbled at Mr Thomas' pullover, leapt over Jodie's head, and disappeared down the road. Mr Thomas was not amused. He didn't put any money in the tin, but grabbed his jacket from the hook behind the door and rushed off down the road, calling 'Bitsy! Bitsy! Daddy's here, don't be frightened!'

Gary and Jodie looked at each other.

'I don't think we'll get any money here,' said Gary. 'Let's carry on. Look, I'll hold the money tin for a while and you can do the talking.'

So as the door of number 24 opened, Jodie gave her biggest smile and said 'Hello, Christine. We've come carol-singing.'

'Oh hello, Jodie,' said Christine. 'What's this all about then?'

Suddenly Jodie's mind went blank. She had forgotten about the hospital. What was she supposed to say now? Then she heard the youth group starting to sing one of her favourite Christmas songs, 'Little donkey', and she knew just what to say.

'It's Mary and Joseph. They're going to Bethlehem. It's a long way, and Mary's going to have a baby any minute. But they've got to get to Bethlehem, 'cos God said the baby would be born there.'

Christine smiled. 'They're singing it so nicely. I'll put some money in your tin. It's for the hospital, is it? A very good cause.'

'Thank you,' said Jodie, and Gary added, 'if you want to hear what happened next to Mary and Joseph, do come to our carol service at church on Sunday.'

'I might do that,' said Christine, and she stayed at the door listening to the singing, as Gary and Jodie went on to number 25.

'You were very good,' whispered Gary. 'You can carry on doing the talking if you like.'

'OK,' whispered back Jodie.

Jodie knew most of the people around the square, at least by sight, so she was quite happy to chat to them. At number 31 the youth group were singing 'Away in a manger', so Jodie told the Smith family all about baby Jesus being born, and having to sleep in an animals' food trough because there wasn't room in the inn. By the time they reached number 39 the carol was 'While shepherds watched their flocks by night'.

'Mrs Saunders who lives here is a bit deaf,' said Jodie, so Gary knocked hard. Mrs Saunders peered round the door. Jodie took a big breath and shouted: 'the ANGELS are TELLING the SHEPHERDS all about baby JESUS being BORN IN BETHLEHEM'.

Mrs Saunders opened the door wide. 'How nice to have someone who speaks up clearly,' she said. 'You're just like a little angel yourself.'

Gary nearly dropped the money tin in surprise at this remark and he couldn't stop laughing as they walked back down the path.

At number 45 Jodie managed to trip over the stone frog in the front garden. She fell into a flower bed, which wasn't very good for the plants, but the damage didn't really show in the dark. Nor did the muddy marks on Jodie's face.

At number 8 (they were nearly round the square and home again) a disaster happened.

'Oh dear, this is Mr Stevens' house,' said Jodie.

'What's the matter?' asked Gary.

'He's very grumpy, worse than Mr Thomas – and he doesn't like children,' said Jodie. She didn't add that Mr Stevens wasn't very keen on teenagers either. 'I think you'd better talk here.'

She looked so worried that Gary said he would. 'Your turn to knock, then,' he said.

Jodie reached up to the bell. Unfortunately, it was half hidden by a very large tinsel wreath, hanging on the door. Jodie managed to knock this as she scrabbled for the bell, and just as the door began to open, the wreath fell right off the door and on to Gary's head. It sort of slid down so that it was dangling round his neck apart from the bit that was hooked up on his right ear. It was not a good moment for Mr Stevens to appear.

Jodie spoke without thinking. 'Hello, Mr Stevens. Doesn't Gary look funny? It's my fault. I knocked the wreath down by mistake. Can you hear the youth club singing? It's all about the wise men. They went to see Jesus, you know, because they saw a star in the sky. God put it there. It showed them the way to Beth...'

'Shh!' said Mr Stevens. He stepped out of the house, down the path, and stood looking at the youth group with their coloured lanterns, as they sang 'We three kings of Orient are'. Mr Stevens stood watching and listening until the end of the carol.

'That song about the wise men used to be my favourite when I was a choirboy. Well, well, well.'

Gary took the opportunity to hang the wreath back on the door, but Jodie had followed Mr Stevens down the path. When the carol was finished, she bravely said, 'We're collecting for the hospital.'

'And I'll put something in your tin,' smiled Mr Stevens. Jodie could hardly believe her eyes and ears.

At last they reached Jodie's next-door neighbours at number 10 (the other side to where they had started). The Jenkins family lived here, and Jodie knew most of them were away; but Granny Susan, the old lady would be in. She had told Louise she'd put some money ready by the door, so Jodie was surprised when she didn't open it. She peered through the letterbox.

'You can't do that,' said Gary, 'it's rude!'

But Jodie had done it – and it was a good thing she had, because she could just see Granny Susan lying at the bottom of the stairs, very still.

'She's hurt, look!'

Gary peered though as well, rude or not, and said 'We need to get help.'

'Daddy will be home by now,' said Jodie. 'He'll know what to do.'

She ran across to her own house and called through the letterbox. Daddy came quickly, opened Granny Susan's door with the spare key they looked after, and had soon called the ambulance.

As the paramedics took Granny Susan off to hospital – 'We're sure she'll be all right soon,' they said cheerfully – Daddy took Jodie indoors to bed and Louise, Gary and the rest of the youth group went off to church to count the money they had collected.

Two evenings later, the whole family went to the carol service at church, and Christine from number 24 joined them. Jodie enjoyed it. She sang all the carols she knew, telling the Christmas story again. But there were two things that made the carol service really special for her. One was that the vicar announced how much money the youth group had collected – a record amount he said. And the other was that – surprise, surprise – Mr Stevens was there. Jodie caught his eye as they were singing 'We three kings of Orient are', and he gave her a big wink.

Marjory Francis

Prayer idea:

> Invite the children or audience to choose their favourite Christmas carol or song. This could be done together or quietly, as individuals. You could choose one or two carols and use them as prayers together, inviting everyone to think about the Christmas story as they sing or say them.

> *'Bethlehem ... you are very important ... From your town will come a leader, who will be like a shepherd for my people Israel.' Matthew 2:6*

Songs featured:
'Once in royal David's city'
'Little donkey'
'Away in a manger'
'While shepherds watched their flocks by night'
'We three kings of Orient are'

The wise man

(Reading time: 10 minutes)

'Please Mrs Timms, Andy's chewing,'

'Oh, Andy,' said Mrs Timms. 'Not again! Pass him the bin, please Chi.'

Andy reluctantly took the half chewed toffee out of his mouth and dropped it into the bin that Chi held out in front of him.

'Have you any more sweets with you?' asked Mrs Timms. Andy fished in his pocket and took out a packet of toffees. He handed them to Mrs Timms.

'Thank you. I'll look after these till home time.'

Mrs Timms sighed. What was she going to do with Andy? Nearly every day she had to tell him off about something, and he was always eating in class. Once he was hiding behind his maths book eating a cold sausage. Another time he disturbed quiet reading with a noisy bag of extra-crunchy crisps. It seemed to be one thing after another, anything instead of getting on with his work.

Mrs Timms knew Andy found his work difficult, and she tried to help him as much as she could. The trouble was he didn't seem to have any confidence in the things he could do. He just thought about the things he couldn't, and gave up. What Andy needs, Mrs Timms thought to herself, is something to help him see that he is just as special as everyone else.

Andy sat at his desk fiddling with his maths book. He struggled to understand the numbers in it. He understood them on their own, it was just when they were all together that he got muddled. Oh, why wasn't he clever like the others? If only he was good at something. He fished around in his pocket to see if there was one toffee that had fallen out of the bag – no, they were all on Mrs Timms' shelf until home time. As he looked up, he caught Mrs Timms' eye. He hastily looked down again at his maths book, but Mrs Timms called softly, 'Andy, come here please.'

'Andy,' said Mrs Timms, as he stood by her desk, 'you know it's our class's turn to perform the play this year, don't you?' Andy nodded. 'I thought we'd do the real Christmas story – you know the one don't you?'

'About baby Jesus? I like that story,' said Andy.

'That's good,' said Mrs Timms. 'Well, you'll remember who's in the story, then. I'd like you to play one of the characters.'

Andy stared at her. He thought hard about who was in the story. He couldn't think of anyone he was like.

'Yes,' went on Mrs Timms, taking a rather deep breath. 'I'd like you to be one of the wise men.'

Andy stared even harder. Had he heard right?

'Me – a wise man?' he stuttered. But I don't feel very wise! he thought to himself.

'I think you'll make a very good one,' said Mrs Timms. 'I thought I might ask James and Kyle to be the others.'

Andy couldn't believe it. He'd never been in a group with James and Kyle before. He really felt he'd suddenly grown quite wise!

'Right,' Mrs Timms was saying, 'that's sorted. Now let's have a go at that maths.'

Over the next few days Andy found he didn't need anything to distract him in class. School work had suddenly become interesting. In English, he and James and Kyle got together to work out what they were going to say as they travelled following the star, and as they came to meet baby Jesus. They wrote the words down, read them to each other, decided they weren't quite right, wrote them again, and so on. It kept them busy for ages.

And then in maths, Andy found he was learning about camels! They were pretending the wise men had to discover how many miles they could travel in a day, and it all depended on how fast the camel walked. They had to know how much camel food to take, and that had to be worked out by knowing how much a camel ate in one day. The numbers on the page began to make sense.

And in technology the task was to make his wise man's gift, a beautifully decorated box to give to the baby Jesus. Only the best will be good enough, thought Andy, who had listened hard to the story. Jesus was a very special baby. The angel said he was God's own Son.

Andy wondered what he could use for his gift. There were boxes in the class junk box, but somehow a cornflake packet was not good enough. He would have to find something special by tomorrow...

And then that evening Gran came back from her Golden Oldies holiday in Florida, bringing a big box of Mr Popple's Gum Jaw Sticky Candies. It was a wonderful box, with a purple band round the edge and a shiny golden bow. It would be just right for his present for Jesus. He would only need to put some decorations over the writing. He put it straight in his school bag to take next morning.

Andy hung his bag on the back of the chair. He was looking forward to showing Mrs Timms the box, but first they had mental maths. If one camel can carry 220 kilograms, how much can three camels carry? As Andy thought hard, his hand absent-mindedly felt in the bag, and then in the box, and before he knew it, he had a Mr Popple's Gum Jaw Sticky Candy in his mouth.

Unfortunately, Sanjay saw him.

'Andy's got sweets, Mrs Timms.'

Andy knew there was no escape. Before Mrs Timms asked, he got out the box and put it on the desk.

'What a lovely box, Andy! Is that for your present for baby Jesus?'

Andy nodded. He couldn't speak. Mr Popple's Gum Jaw Sticky Candy had done its work and his teeth were stuck together.

'Well, I'll keep the sweets in a bag for you, and you can decorate your box this afternoon.' She smiled at Andy, and he smiled back, as far as Mr Popple's Gum Jaw Sticky Candy would allow.

The next couple of days were very busy. There were costumes to finish and the hall to decorate, as well as the final rehearsals. At last the day for the play came. Everyone was excited – especially Andy. His mum was taking time off work, and Gran was coming to watch too.

The class got ready in record time. There were still 15 minutes to go as Mrs Timms looked around at them, waiting in their places to be called from the hall. She felt very proud of everyone. They really did look the part! Mary and Joseph looked proud and a bit nervous too – probably just like the real Mary and Joseph. The shepherds carried crooks and left bits of straw trailing behind them as they walked around! The angels' tinsel halos glittered in the light. And the wise men looked – wise. Mrs Timms smiled at Andy. How well he had done! He had written and learnt his words, and thanks to the camels, his maths was coming on a treat.

Then she remembered. She had never given Andy back his bag of Mr Popple's Gum Jaw Sticky Candies.

'I'm sorry, Andy,' she said, reaching up to the shelf. 'I'll give them to you now in case I forget later.'

Andy looked at the bag in surprise. He'd forgotten about them too. But it felt like a special occasion and he had an idea.

'Can I share them out round the class?' he asked.

'Of course you can,' said Mrs Timms, 'as long as everyone promises not to eat them before the play.'

Andy went round the room giving everyone a Mr Popple's Gum Jaw Sticky Candy. When he got back to his place there were just three left.

'There must have been 32 in there,' he said, ''cos I haven't had one yet. And you haven't either,' he continued, putting one on Mrs Timms desk.

There was one Mr Popple's Gum Jaw Sticky Candy left. He knew exactly what he was going to do with it. He opened his beautifully decorated box and slipped it inside, just as the headmaster put his head round the door to say 'time to go!'

Andy's mum and gran beamed as Andy crossed the stage. Andy held his head high as he walked proudly between James and Kyle. He reached the manger. He forgot it was just a doll lying there. He imagined it was the real baby Jesus, and he was giving him the best gift he had. He knelt down, put his precious gift beside the baby, and said 'This is for you, Jesus.'

Marjory Francis

Prayer idea:

Dear God, the wise men gave Jesus the most precious things that they could. Help us to give you our best gifts, too. Amen.

'When the [wise] men went into the house and saw the child with Mary, his mother, they knelt down and worshipped him. They took out their gifts of gold, frankincense, and myrrh and gave them to him.' Matthew 2:11

The Glooms and the shortest day

(Reading time: 10 minutes)

Storytelling tips: the story will work well if you read Grandfather Gloom's speech in a gloomy voice. If it is practical, you could try darkening the room and then turning lights on at the end, when Joshua Gloom sees the Christmas tree.

It is quite possible that you have never met a Gloom. Unless you spend a lot of time in the dark, and can see in the dark, you certainly won't have met one.

Glooms are strange creatures that live their lives keeping out of the light. They live in cupboards and attics, in coal-holes and under floorboards. Some Glooms even live underground. The one thing that they all hate is light.

If, by some strange chance, you saw a Gloom, you would notice one very special thing about it. They have two feet and four hands. The feet are used for walking or tunnelling. The lower set of hands is used for feeling and eating and scratching. The upper set of hands is always held over their eyes. This is just in case they should come out by mistake into the light.

It isn't much fun being a Gloom. Because they live in the dark, they can't see anything, so they have to do everything by touch. They search for food by touch, they comb their fur by touch and clean their teeth by touch. They never clear up the mess in their bedrooms. (Maybe that is your idea of fun!)

Glooms live in big families. The leader is usually the oldest Gloom, who also teaches the Gloomlets. The Gloomlets go to Gloom School every day for the National Gloom Curriculum. The younger ones are in Gloom Stage One and the older ones, yes – you've guessed, are in Gloom Stage Two.

What I am about to tell you took place just before Christmas. A group of young Gloomlets were sitting in a cellar listening to their grandfather.

'Gloomlets,' he said in his rather gloomy voice, 'today is a very happy day for all Glooms. It is the shortest day in the year. It is the day we enjoy the longest darkness. To celebrate the day we will sing the Gloom National Anthem. Please stand to attention. I will sing the first verse and you will then repeat it with me.'

Grandfather Gloom sang the following words:

> In this belief all Glooms unite,
> Welcome dark and drive out light.
> Stick to black and murky places,
> There to show our Gloomish faces.
> This is the song we sing as one,
> Banish moon and banish sun,
> To keep the darkness all around,
> The Gloomish future's underground.

The Gloomlets joined in and sang the other verses, which were even sillier.

They had just finished singing the Gloom National Anthem when Granny Gloom felt her way in. Holding her hand, the lower one of course, was a young Gloom.

'Grandfather Gloom,' said Granny Gloom, 'I have a new student for your school. His name is Joshua Gloomlet.'

Little did Grandfather Gloom know it but Joshua was about to change their lives for ever. Of course, as everyone was in the dark, Grandfather Gloom couldn't see Joshua.

'Welcome, Joshua Gloomlet,' said Grandfather Gloom. 'Come and join our party on the shortest day of the year. You're just in time for a piece of Shortest Day Cake.'

If you've never had Shortest Day Cake you won't know that it is baked with black flour, with soot-flavoured icing sugar on the top. Of course Glooms never have candles – so there weren't any to blow out.

'It's time for Assembly,' said Grandfather Gloom. 'Today, our special day, I am going to tell you a story.'

The Gloomlets settled down to listen. Grandfather Gloom cleared his throat.

'This is the story of a very famous Gloom called Tone of Dark. Tone lived many years ago long before electric lights made our lives so miserable. In those days humans used candles and lanterns to provide the light they needed. One day Tone was hiding in a cupboard, waiting for the dark, when a human came into the room. Very bravely Tone looked through a crack in the cupboard door and watched as the human lit a candle. At that moment another human came into the room. Even though it meant Tone had to look at the candle flame, he noticed that as the other human came in, the flame flickered and nearly went out.

'Tone then began experimenting. When he was on his own he lit another candle. He jumped around in front of it and watched as it flickered. The jumping disturbed the dust and Tone sneezed. At once the candle went out. Tone now knew that blowing on flames would put them out.

'Tone shared the good news with other Glooms. Soon brave young Glooms were blowing out candles everywhere.

'Humans were baffled. And it was all because of Tone of Dark. Sadly we soon discovered that you cannot blow out an electric light. But we Glooms will never forget Tone of Dark.'

The Gloomlets clapped.

'Thank you, Grandfather Gloom, that was a lovely story,' said Gertie Gloomlet.

Joshua Gloomlet sat through the Assembly thinking about the story. He had been brought up to ask questions if he didn't understand something. His parents were quite exhausted by some of his questions – like, 'Why should we eat cabbage?' and 'If we live in the dark why do we bother brushing our fur? No one can see what we look like!' A question was beginning to bubble up in Joshua's brain. It was a very big question. It was the sort of question which might get him into trouble. Suddenly it burst out.

'Why do we live in the dark?'

Grandfather Gloom was badly shaken. Nobody had ever asked him that. He thought for a moment and then answered.

'Because we have always lived in the dark.'

'But,' said Joshua Gloomlet, 'we don't have to. We could take our hands away from our eyes. Then we would see the light!'

'Don't even suggest it!' shouted Grandfather Gloom. 'That would mean a whole new world – a new way of life – a change of direction. No sensible, intelligent, thinking Gloom would ever want to live in the light.'

But, thought Joshua, I'm a sensible, intelligent, thinking Gloom and I want to live in the light. So during break time Joshua felt his way towards the door. Nobody saw him slip through it. As he climbed the cellar stairs the light grew brighter. Slowly Joshua slid his higher pair of hands away from his eyes. He blinked several times and looked around. He could see! What a difference. It was a whole new world.

The passage at the top of the cellar steps led into a large room. Standing in the room was a Christmas tree. Joshua stopped. He couldn't believe what he saw. He opened and closed his eyes. The lights on the tree were dazzling. It was the most beautiful thing he had ever seen or imagined in his whole life. There were so many colours – colours he never knew were possible. And there on the top of the tree was a bright star. Joshua stood with his mouth wide open and stared in amazement. Now he knew light was right.

Brian Ogden

Prayer idea:

> Thank you, God, for shining the light of your Son, Jesus, into a dark world on that first Christmas. Help us to welcome his light into our hearts and homes at this time of year, and always. Amen.

> *'The light keeps shining in the dark, and darkness has never put it out ... The true light that shines on everyone was coming into the world.' John 1:5,9*

Busy night in Bethlehem

[To be sung to the tune of 'God rest ye merry, gentlemen']

Move over, mate, I need more room,
You're hogging all the sheet,
And did you know you snore a lot
And you have freezing feet?
I never thought I'd share a bed
With men I chanced to meet.
Oh, why did I come to Bethlehem? (Should'a stayed home...)
Oh, why did I come to Bethlehem?

Now, hush that noise, we're trying to sleep.
We've had a busy day.
We've done our best to find a space
For all who want to stay.
Some people have no bed at all –
They're sleeping in the hay.
Oh, who'd run an inn in Bethlehem? (Should'a sheared sheep...)
Oh, who'd run an inn in Bethlehem?

Now let me help, you poor young girl;
Your plight I can't ignore.
I have three children of my own;
I've done all this before,
Though I have never given birth
Upon a stable floor
Oh, who'd bear a babe in Bethlehem? (In a cowshed...)
Oh, who'd bear a babe in Bethlehem?

I'll leave you now, you need to sleep.
You've had a busy night.
Your babe is sleeping soundly now
And what a glorious sight!
Praise be to God, this lovely child
Is bathed in golden light!
Someone special is born in Bethlehem! (Who can he be?)
Someone special is born in Bethlehem!

Gillian Ellis

Maximus Mouse's unexpected visitors

(Reading time: 10 minutes)

It was Christmas Eve and Maximus couldn't remember a colder Christmas. The wind was blowing hard against the vestry windows and there were flakes of snow in the wind. It was bitterly cold even though the heating was on for the Christmas Day services. Maximus had given his presents to Patrick, Paula and the mouselings. He had sent cards to Barnabas the church bat, to Herbert the hedgehog, and to Robert and his family of rabbits.

Maximus was actually feeling quite proud of himself. For once he was ready for the great day. He had done his shopping and bought all the food he would need. Usually he had Christmas lunch with Patrick and Paula but they had gone away and Maximus was on his own.

There were old films on the television – *Mousy Poppins* about a nursemouse who could do magical things, *The Snowmouse* and *Soot Black* and the *Seven Mouselings*. He had seen them all before.

'Might as well go to bed,' he said to the empty vestry. 'Then when I wake up I can open my pressies. But it's going to be a lonely Christmas on my own.'

Maximus snuggled down under his duvet. He had managed to find several tissues and a real handkerchief so his bed was really warm and comfortable. Very soon he was asleep and snoring quietly.

Half an hour later there was a strange noise. It sounded as though somebody was trying to get into the vestry through Maximus' special hole. At first the noise didn't wake Maximus but as it got louder he stirred.

Suddenly he was wide awake. There was definitely somebody in his vestry. He lay quite still on his bed and listened hard. There were two somebodies – he could hear them whispering. Were they burglars after his Christmas presents? Was he going to be mouse-napped and held to ransom?

After ten minutes he could stand it no longer. They were still there and he had to know what they were doing. He got up very quietly and found the little torch he kept under the bed. He turned it on and shone the beam round the vestry.

There on the carpet by the vicar's desk, holding their paws in front of their eyes to shield them from the light, were two strange mice. They looked very cold and very wet and very tired.

'And just what do you think you are doing?' asked Maximus, sounding braver than he felt. 'This is my vestry – you are tresmousing!'

'We're looking for somewhere to stay,' said one of the mice. 'You see, my wife is going to have mouselings very soon. We are mouseholeless and it's freezing outside. Please, please may we stay?'

Maximus scratched his head with his paw. They looked so unhappy that he couldn't throw them out.

'Yes, er... of course. I expect you're hungry,' he went on. 'Let's see what I can find.'

He looked at his Christmas lunch of carol sheet pasta with candle wax sauce. Perhaps that would cheer them up. He soon warmed it and gave it to the visitors. He made some stinging nettle tea and sat with them as they all warmed their paws round the mugs. Maximus put his duvet gently round the lady mouse's shoulders.

'My name's Jo and my wife's name is Maria. The house we were living in was knocked down to build a new road. We've been desperately searching for somewhere to have our first mouselings.'

'It is so kind of you, er... Mr... um?' said Maria.

'Maximus,' said Maximus. 'I'm the mousekeeper in this church. I sort of keep an eye on things for the vicar.'

'Mr Maximus, it really is very good of you to let us stay.'

Maximus found some more warm things for Jo and Maria and they all settled down to sleep. It was quite late on Christmas morning before Maximus woke up again. He yawned and stretched his paws and started to think about what had happened in the night. Then he heard a funny little noise. It was the sort of tiny squeaking noise that Paula's mouselings sometimes made.

Maximus jumped out of bed and scampered over to the vicar's desk. There, in an open drawer, was a very proud looking Jo, a tired but happy Maria, and six tiny baby mouselings.

'Maximus, meet your honorary grandmouselings,' said Jo with a big smile.

Maximus was squeakless. It was just amazing to see the tiny mouselings all nestling up to their mother. Their eyes were shut and they wore very little fur. Maximus' duvet was tucked around them and they seemed warm and happy.

'Well,' said Maximus, 'I just don't know what to say. It's quite a surprise to wake up to find six new mouselings in my vestry. Congratulations. Have you thought of any names yet?'

'There are two boys and four girls,' said Jo. 'We thought, if you didn't mind, we could call the oldest boy Maximus, after you, and the younger one Thomas. The girls will be named after our mothers, Susan and Sally, and after the children's grandparents, Eleanor and Patricia.'

'I should be very honoured,' said Maximus.

'I hope you weren't too lonely without us,' said Paula, when the family came home on Boxing Day.

'Yes, we thought about you being on your own,' said Patrick.

'I wasn't on my own,' said Maximus. 'I had a wonderful Christmas. You see, I had some rather unexpected visitors and they had babies and I'm an honorary grandmouse.'

Maximus told Patrick and Paula the whole story of how Jo and Maria had arrived and how their babies had been born in the vestry as they were homeless.

'It's very strange because that's not really the end,' said Maximus. 'Just after they had gone to look for a home of their own I went into the church. Lying on the floor under the choir stalls was a carol sheet. I was just about to eat it when some words caught my eye. They were these. They were so nice I learnt them:

Away in a manger, no crib for a bed,
The little Lord Jesus laid down his sweet head.
The stars in the bright sky looked down where he lay,
The little Lord Jesus asleep on the hay.

It sort of reminded me of what happened on Christmas Day in my vestry.'

Brian Ogden

Prayer idea:

Loving Father, you gave us Jesus at Christmas time. Help us to know him, to love him and to serve him, every day in the year. Amen.

Joseph's story

(Reading time: 10 minutes)

The Emperor had ordered everyone to go back to their home towns. It seemed he wanted to have everybody counted, to see how much tax he could collect. Mary and I knew we would have to go back to Bethlehem. It was not an easy journey from Nazareth: it would take us over ten days to walk. With Mary expecting the baby it was going to be difficult for her, so we'd have to take it slowly.

Our journey took longer than we thought. By the time we got to Bethlehem the village was crowded, and the inn was full of travellers like us. It seemed everyone had relations staying with them, too. We knew nobody; at least, not well enough to get a place to stay, so it all looked pretty hopeless. Then somebody suggested an animal shelter nearby. It was dry and out of the wind, and a place where we could be together. I had to spend some of our coins on food, but at least they didn't charge us for the shelter.

After our journey we soon settled in, which is just as well, as the baby came very soon. He was a tiny bundle, all sort of screwed-up looking. I felt silly and just said, 'Hello Jesus,' only my voice sounded a bit odd. There was some straw in the feeding basket, so we settled the little thing in there while Mary slept. I just sat and watched. I couldn't take my eyes off him, even though all he did was sleep.

The animals were smelly and the place was dirty, but all that mattered was the three of us: Mary, me and Jesus, our boy, our baby. I held him for a while, just gazing at him. I knew I wasn't his father, but I was going to be his dad, teach him his prayers and all about God. Maybe I could teach him to be a carpenter. That would be good. I thought that if he had a trade he'd never go hungry.

After a while I put him back in the feeding trough, nothing like the cradle I had made for him, but he seemed happy enough. He soon settled to sleep again, babies seem to do a lot of that. I watched for a bit, then I must have dozed off myself because I was disturbed by a scrabbling sound. I thought at first it was one of the goats trying to get back inside, then I heard a voice.

'We've come to see the baby, please,' they said, and slowly a face appeared. I could see no harm so invited him in. He was so awkward, he seemed almost afraid and very shy. As he came in I noticed some others standing behind him, so I went across and asked them all in. Like their friend they stood around wide-eyed and amazed. You would have thought that they had never seen a baby before. I started to get a bit worried; they were ordinary looking people, just like us, but they were so very quiet, it was odd.

Mary lifted the baby out of the feeding trough and held him so they could all see. Then, one by one, they knelt down. There was almost total silence, apart from the noise of the animals. It was very odd, but I wasn't afraid now.

One of them said, 'The angel sent us.'

I didn't say anything. To be quite honest I couldn't think what to say. The only angels I knew were the ones who'd told Mary and me about the baby. Now it seemed angels were appearing to all sorts of people – not that I minded.

'Told us we'd find him sleeping in a feeding rack, all

wrapped up,' added another one in a whisper.

'They told us not to be afraid,' added a third. 'I was, though. I'd never seen an angel before.'

'It wasn't just the one angel,' explained another. 'The sky seemed full of them, lots of them; brighter than the moon, brighter than the sun even. The whole of our valley was lit up.'

One of them, I think he must have been the oldest, started to tell the story about how an angel had sent them to see us. He'd hardly started before someone interrupted, adding a little detail. Then someone else would start to tell us what happened, only to be interrupted again. I really found it quite difficult to follow, but my Mary, she just sat there holding the baby and smiling.

In the end the oldest looking one asked if he could hold the little one, just for a bit. Mary didn't mind in the least, she didn't even suggest that he ought to be careful. She just passed over our Jesus as if he was going to his grandfather or something. Everyone settled down a bit then. The old man sat with his back against the wall with his feet stuck out in front of him, and several of the others crowded round. The baby wriggled one hand free, then the other and grabbed hold of his finger. As he waved his arms around he pulled the old man's hand this way and that. This really made their day – it set them all off chuckling and laughing. I left them to it and went outside just to look at the stars. I had hardly a chance to look at the sky before a quiet shadow joined me.

'I'm called Seth,' he said. 'That's my dad with the baby, the others are my younger brothers.'

We stood a while in silence.

'Forgive me asking,' said Seth politely, 'but do you understand what's going on?'

I said nothing, waiting for him to continue.

'I've never seen an angel before, though I heard about the

ones that appeared to Father Abraham.' He paused and rubbed his hands against his face. 'We're nobody special, just shepherds, though we like to think we could be related to kings, way back. Well, King David looked after sheep, and he came from round here.'

He stopped talking and turned to face me.

'The angel told us that our Saviour was born, the Christ, the Lord, the promised One, the Messiah. But you're not that different from us, and that animal shelter is no place for God's promised One to be born. It's all so very ordinary.'

I paused, thinking how to answer, then I just said, 'A sky full of singing angels – that's not so very ordinary. I only got to see one, and there was no singing, either.' I stopped again, not really sure how to continue. 'Can you remember the angels' song? What did they sing?'

Seth screwed up his eyes and recited, just like a piece of the Law he had learnt at synagogue: '"Praise God in heaven! Peace on earth to everyone who pleases God." That was what they sang, over and over, all different voices, some high, some low. I've never heard anything like it. I was surprised there weren't crowds from Jerusalem come to see what the noise was. It was amazing – sort of special.' He stopped speaking and just gazed at the stars.

I looked up at the sky myself, then I said, 'It sounds as if you know about as much as I do. I don't think I could explain it any more than you can. I feel just like someone caught up in the middle of a story. Maybe I'll never see the end, but I'm happy to trust God.'

We were silent then, each thinking our own thoughts and looking up at the star-filled sky.

It was getting colder, so we went back in. Seth went across to join his brothers. Our Jesus was being passed around now. Each person held him for a few minutes, then passed him on.

The old man, Seth's father, said a blessing and then Seth, who was the last to hold him, gave him a kiss before handing him back to Mary. That seemed the signal for them all to go. They left quietly, but once they were outside one of them started to sing, then the others joined in. I could hear their voices as they sang their way back to the fields and I recognised the words. It seems their angels had taught them a new song. It sounded good.

Michael Wells

Prayer idea:

> Dear God, when the shepherds saw Jesus on that first Christmas, they knew he was a very special baby. Help us to worship you just as they did, and to welcome you in everything we do this Christmas. Amen.
>
> *'As the shepherds returned to their sheep, they were praising God and saying wonderful things about him.' Luke 2:20*

Pass the parcel

(Reading time: 10 minutes)

It all began because Ginny had hurt her leg.

'Sol,' said Jock, 'you live near Ginny, don't you? With her leg in plaster she won't be able to get to Sunday Gang again before Christmas and I thought it would be good to give her a present. Could you ask your mum if you could deliver it to her?'

'OK,' said Sol. 'I could do it on my way home.'

Everybody wrote their names on a label around a big 'To Ginny' and Jock stuck it on the parcel.

'There you go,' he said. 'Thanks, Sol.'

Sol took the parcel. He looked at the wrapping paper. It had funny snowmen all over it and they were telling silly jokes like 'Knock, knock. Who's there? Icy. Icy who? I see you through the keyhole and I'm not opening the door.' No wonder they were laughing, thought Sol, chuckling too. That'll cheer Ginny up with her bad leg.

Sol felt the parcel carefully. It was an interesting shape, sort of flat but very bumpy. Sol wondered what was in it. Jock had said there were 'bits and bobs', whatever they were.

He rang Ginny's doorbell and her mum opened the door.

'I've got a present from Sunday Gang for Ginny,' he said.

'Come in,' said Ginny's mum. 'She'll be glad to see you. She's feeling a bit sorry for herself.'

'Hi, Ginny!' said Sol cheerfully. 'Why didn't the snowman smile?'

'Hi, Sol,' said Ginny. 'I don't know.'

'Because it's snow joke,' said Sol, handing her the parcel. 'Plenty more jokes for you to read yourself. It's from Sunday Gang.'

'Oh thanks, Sol,' said Ginny, looking more cheerful. 'I've been so bored here all by myself.'

Sol stayed for a while and they read all the jokes, giggling together. Sol wrote his favourite on the hard white plaster on Ginny's leg, then said he'd better be getting home.

'I'd better not open the parcel till Christmas,' said Ginny, so Sol never did discover what the 'bits and bobs' were. Still, he'd passed the parcel, and that was a good job done.

'Oh Sol,' said Ginny's mum as she let him out of the front door, 'are you going to Alastair's party this afternoon?'

'Yes,' said Sol.

'Could you take this present from Ginny? She can't make it, of course.'

'Sure,' said Sol.

So he left Ginny's house carrying another parcel.

This parcel was very different — flat but not bumpy. Sol wondered what was in it. It's obviously something in a box, he thought. He shook it and it rattled a bit. Better not shake it too hard — it might get broken.

Alastair had a party at the church hall every year just before Christmas. There was usually an entertainer as well as games, and the food was always fantastic.

Alastair's dad welcomed Sol at the door of the hall.

'Good to see you, Sol. Go straight through to the other room. Mr Bone is just about to start his show.'

'Oh good,' said Sol. 'Here, I've brought some presents for Alastair.' He gave his own present and Ginny's to Alastair's dad, who thanked him and put them on a table by a little Christmas tree. It was obvious that Alastair wasn't going to open Ginny's present now, and Sol never did discover what was in it. Still, he'd passed the parcel, and that was a good job done.

Sol went into the other room where there was a buzz of excitement. Mr Bone was a very funny clown who did magic tricks too. Soon his show was in full swing, and all the children were doubled up with laughter. At one point one of the jokes was familiar and Sol thought 'Mr Bone's been reading that snowman wrapping paper', but Mr Bone told it in such a funny way that Sol roared with laughter all over again.

Too soon it was time to go home, tummy full of lovely food and pockets stuffed with prizes from the games. Mum came to fetch Sol, and as they were leaving, Alastair's dad said:

'You go past Alastair's granny's house, don't you? She wasn't well enough today to come out in the cold wind, but she'd love something from the party. Could you take her some goodies?'

So Sol left the party carrying a present for Alastair's gran.

Sol looked at the plastic plate as he sat in the back of the car. It was tightly covered with foil, and he wondered what was underneath it – a chocolate crispie or a sausage roll? A little iced bun or some burger-flavoured crisps? And surely there would be a big slice of the delicious Christmas gateau! He read the label: 'To Gran with love from Alastair' and smiled at Alastair's picture of a very wobbly Christmas tree with Mary, Joseph and baby Jesus beside it.

'Oh Sol, how kind of you,' smiled Alastair's granny. She took the plate, but she didn't look under the foil, so Sol never did discover what was on it. Still, he'd passed the parcel, and that was a good job done.

'Was it a good party?' asked Alastair's granny. 'I was sorry to miss it this year.'

'It was great, Mrs Flint,' said Sol.

'Is there anything we can do for you while we're here?' asked Sol's mum.

'Well, since you ask,' said Mrs Flint, 'could you take this little gift to a friend of mine? Jim Hatch.'

'Mr Hatch lives just next door to us,' said Sol. 'I sometimes take his dog out for a walk. I'll pop round with it as soon as I get home.'

So Sol left Alastair's granny's carrying another parcel.

'Don't drop it,' said Mum. 'I think it might be breakable.'

Yes, thought Sol. It feels like a jar of some sort. Perhaps it's jam or marmalade. He looked at the paper round it. It had stars and angels all over it and some sparkly stuff to make them shine. Sol remembered that a star and angels came in the Christmas story, and it made him think of something else.

'I feel like a wise man, Mum,' he said, 'all these presents to deliver.'

They both laughed.

'I don't think there's been any gold, frankincense or myrrh,' said Mum.

Mr Hatch was delighted with his present.

'Mrs Flint makes the most delicious lemon curd,' he said. 'I think it might be that.' But he didn't open the parcel to find out, so Sol never did discover what was in it. Still, he'd passed the parcel, and that was a good job done.

Then Mr Hatch said: 'And now there's something you can do for me.'

Sol and Mum looked at each other and grinned.

'You'll be seeing Tommy, my grandson, at school, won't you?'

Sol nodded. He knew what was coming.

'Could you take this then please?' He handed Sol a carrier bag. Sol took it.

'Thanks ever so much,' said Mr Hatch.

So Sol left Mr Hatch's house with yet another present for someone else.

On the way to school next day Sol sat in the back of the car and looked at the carrier bag. It was a very nice one. It didn't have the name of a shop on it. Instead there was a fat cat with a huge smile, wearing a bow tie with holly on it. Next to the cat a bulging stocking was hanging up. The words said: 'Stocking up for Christmas.' Sol thought that was very clever. He hoped Tommy would like the present inside.

Tommy did. At least, he was very pleased to get it, and said he'd take it home to keep for Christmas morning. So Sol never did discover what was in Tommy's present. Still, he'd passed the parcel, and that was a good job done.

Sol was very pleased too that Tommy didn't give him anything in exchange. At last there was nothing else to take on to someone else!

The next day, Tommy hunted Sol down in the playground. He held the cat carrier bag in his hand. Oh no, thought Sol, not another delivery!

'I'm really sorry,' said Tommy. 'I didn't realise there was a present for you in the bag too.'

'Was there?' asked Sol. 'A present for me?' He looked inside the bag. There was a little flat parcel labelled 'To Sol from Mr Hatch'.

'Oh, great! Thanks, Tommy.'

'There's just one more thing,' said Tommy. He held out a rather crumpled envelope. 'Do you think you could deliver this thank-you note to my grandad?'

Sol had a picture in his mind of delivering endless thank you letters. He took a deep breath.

'Sure,' said Sol, 'anytime!'

On Christmas morning Sol opened Mr Hatch's bag. At last,

he thought, the parcel has stopped with me. He unwrapped the little flat present and found *The world's funniest joke book.* Oh great! he thought. I can tell Ginny lots more jokes. And then he remembered — that was how it had all begun. Still, he had passed the parcels, and it was all a good job done!

Marjory Francis

Prayer idea:

Thank you, God, that we can celebrate Christmas by giving each other presents. Thank you for the best gift of all, the one you gave us — your Son, Jesus. Amen.

The Christmas C

Can you count the number of words beginning with 'c' in this poem? You have to listen very carefully...

> The Cake and Cards and Choccies (lots!),
> The Candles, Crackers, Chimney-pots,
> And Claus now brings us season's greeting
> By squeezing through the Central heating.
> There's Church and Chapel Celebration,
> Carols sung throughout the nation,
> Crib and Cream and Chestnuts roasting
> Cosy firelight, toes a-toasting.
> The greatest C that's in this rhyme?
> The Christ-child, born at Christmas time.

Gillian Ellis

(Answer: 18)

Dad for Christmas

(Reading time: 10 minutes)

Nikita wasn't listening. It's not that that the Assembly was boring, but simply that she had something else on her mind. She was thinking about the last time she'd seen her dad.

Nikita's dad was in the Navy. She hadn't seen him since the summer holidays and she'd lost count of how many weeks had gone by since then. Now they were back at school after half-term. It would soon be Christmas and Nikita couldn't imagine Christmas without her dad.

'So, are you going to have a go?' whispered Molly, Nikita's best friend.

'Have a go at what?' whispered back Nikita.

'You were dreaming again,' giggled Molly. 'Mrs Kent was talking about a writing competition.'

They sang a song, listened to all the notices about litter in the playground and mud in the gym and went back to their classroom.

'What's this competition, then?' asked Nikita.

'There's going to be a prize for the best poem,' said Molly. 'The title is, "What I want for Christmas".'

Nikita thought about it. There was only one thing she wanted for Christmas – her dad home safely. But could she write a poem about that? Would it count?

'I hope lots of you will enter the competition,' said Mr Frost,

Nikita's teacher.

Nikita lived with her mum and Kane, her younger brother. Her dad had been in the Navy for as long as Nikita could remember. It was fantastic when he was home but she missed him badly when he was at sea. This time his ship, a destroyer, was in a dangerous part of the world. Nikita and her mum watched the television news every evening when Kane was in bed. Once they had seen Dad's ship not far from the war area. Dad usually phoned once a week but he couldn't tell them much as everything had to be kept secret.

After tea Nikita found an old exercise book and started to write her poem. Wouldn't it be fantastic if she won! Then she could show it to Dad when he came home.

> My dad is far away at sea,
> Miles and miles from his family.
> He's a sailor in the Royal Navy...

Then there was a problem – she couldn't think of a word to rhyme with 'Navy' apart from 'gravy'. And that didn't seem right. Perhaps if she left out the 'Royal Navy' bit it would be easier.

> He's been a sailor for years and years,
> He's really brave and has no fears.

She read the last line again and wasn't sure that it was true. When she had been frightened by a huge Alsatian dog in the park she had asked Dad if he was ever scared. She had never forgotten what he said.

'Yes, I have been. I've been terrified by big storms at sea when the waves break right over the front of the ship. Being frightened isn't wrong – it's what you do when you are frightened that counts.'

So she couldn't put 'has no fears'. Writing poems wasn't as easy as she thought.

At that moment the phone rang. She raced her mum to pick it up. It was Dad! It was hard to hear him as there were a lot of crackling noises. She just managed to hear him say, 'Lots of love, Nikita' before she handed the phone to her mum. Perhaps next time she could tell him about the surprise – that is if she won. But that meant actually finishing the poem.

Molly called for Nikita on the way to school the next morning.

'Can you think of any words that rhyme with "pony"?' Molly asked. 'It's for that poem competition – I'm going to win it!'

Nikita didn't answer at first – she was having enough trouble finding her own words. But Molly was a friend, so she tried to help.

'What about "macaroni"?' she said, laughing. 'Macaroni rhymes with pony.'

Molly didn't seem to think 'macaroni' was funny. When they reached the playground they found that almost everyone in their class was entering the competition. I don't stand a chance of winning, Nikita thought glumly.

Later that morning in their English lesson Mr Frost spoke about the poem competition.

'I know lots of you have rushed into writing a poem,' he said, 'but good poems need to be thought about. You must think carefully about the choice of words. It might help to read some other poems before you write yours.'

So after tea, Nikita looked on the bookshelf and found a book of poems. Inside the front cover she read these words: 'School Poetry Prize 1975. Awarded to Emmanuel Campbell'. It was her dad's book! Nikita worked it out – Dad must have been the same age then that she was now. Nikita was more determined than ever to win. She curled up in the big arm chair and began to read. Dad had ticked some of the poems – they must have been his favourites.

Reading the poems made Nikita think and she went to find the old exercise book. The page where she had started the night before was covered in felt-tip pen. Kane had used it for drawing a picture! She had to start again. This time the words came more easily. Christmas was about a special family in Bethlehem – so perhaps that was the place to start. And this is the poem that Nikita wrote:

> What did Mary want for Christmas?
> A wonderful baby son.
> When Jesus was born, Joseph knew
> A family had begun.
>
> What do we all want for Christmas?
> Mum and Nikita and Kane,
> To wake up and know that Dad is here,
> A family once again.
>
> What do I really want for Christmas,
> To make it the best I've had?
> Not presents or lots and lots to eat –
> But a great big hug from Dad.

Nikita showed the poem to her mum before she went to bed.

Her mum read it through twice. She put her arms round Nikita and gave her a hug.

'That's just how I feel too,' she said quietly.

The next night Nikita wrote out the poem in her best writing. At school she handed it in to Mr Frost.

'Good luck, Nikita,' he said. 'We won't know who's won

until the day school finishes for Christmas.'

The next few days went very slowly. The news on the television wasn't very good and they didn't hear from Dad for nearly a fortnight. On the last day of term the whole school came together for a special Assembly. Standing next to Mrs Kent was Councillor James, the Chair of the Governors.

'I hope I've won,' whispered Molly.

'We have had a very difficult job choosing the best poem,' said Mrs Kent. 'Councillor James has very generously decided to give three prizes as there were so many excellent entries.'

Molly gave a little squeak before Mrs Kent continued.

'The third prize goes to Connor Finnigan from Class H. The second prize goes to Molly Webster from Class F.'

Nikita looked at the floor. There was no chance of winning first prize so she stopped listening.

The next thing she knew, Molly was shaking her.

'YOU'VE WON FIRST PRIZE!'

Connor, Molly and Nikita went to the front as everyone clapped. They shook hands with Councillor James and Connor and Molly were each given a Book Token. Then Councillor James handed Nikita a book. It was a big book of poems. Inside Nikita read, 'School Poetry Prize: Awarded to Nikita Campbell'.

On Christmas morning Nikita was woken up by Kane bouncing on her bed.

'Is it time to go into Mum's yet?' he said. 'I want to see my presents!'

Nikita and Kane pushed open their parents' door. Something was different. There were two lumps under the duvet! One of them sat up.

'Happy Christmas, you two,' said Dad. 'Now come and give me a hug.'

Brian Ogden

Prayer ideas:

Thank you, God, for the good times we can have with our families at Christmas. Thank you for lovely food, fun and holidays to spend together. Please help us to have a happy time with our families this Christmas! Amen.

Dear God, we know that lots of people are away from their families this Christmas. Please help them to know that you care about them and are with them. Amen.

The legend of the spider's web

(Reading time: 10 minutes)

Two thousand years ago, on the night Jesus was born, the animals in the stable were discussing what gifts they could give him.

'I'll give him my hay to sleep on, and my manger for his bed,' said the donkey.

'I shall keep him warm with my breath,' said the ox.

The yard dogs lay across the stable door and growled, 'We shall protect him from harm. No one will get past us!'

The stable cat stretched sleepily and said, 'I shall sing him a lullaby,' and she purred a warm, comfortable, furry song for him.

High up in the rafters a little spider watched and listened.

'Whatever can I give to the baby king?' she said sadly to herself. 'People are frightened if I come close to them, and I have no gifts, anyway.'

Later that night shepherds arrived, bringing a gift of a lamb for the baby. Mary and Joseph were so happy with the new baby. The little spider watched it all. If only she could think of something she could give to the baby she would feel really happy.

One morning the little spider heard Cousin Ben telling Joseph that there was an empty workshop in the town. It would need some repairs done to it, but if Joseph was interested there was a small house attached that could probably be rented too. Mary and Joseph seemed very pleased to hear this news and Mary told the baby that they would soon be moving out of the stable to a home of their own.

'Joseph can go back to work as a carpenter,' she told Jesus, 'and maybe one day you will be a carpenter, too.'

The little spider sighed. 'But I don't want them to go. I'll be all alone again up here in the dark.'

'Why not come with us?' asked the donkey. 'Hide in one of my carrying bags – I'm sure you'd not be noticed and I don't think you'd be too heavy for me to carry!'

So when the family moved to their new home the little spider moved too. She made herself a new nest above the door in Joseph's workshop where she could watch him work – and the first thing he made was a lovely wooden cradle for the baby.

Days passed and became weeks and months. The baby grew into a toddler and loved to play among the wood shavings on the workshop floor. The little spider spun her webs and imagined what she would have made for him if only she could – a soft warm shawl, a swinging hammock up among the rafters, a net to keep the flies away from him when he slept.

'I just wish I could give him something,' she said to the donkey.

The donkey nodded calmly.

'You'll think of something,' he replied, 'you'll see.'

That night, just as Joseph was closing up the workshop, something very strange happened. There was a great commotion out in the street – harness bells, dogs barking, and strangers' voices. The door opened. Outlined in the brilliance of starlight stood richly-dressed strangers from far-away lands. They came in and knelt among the sawdust at Jesus' feet, calling him their king.

The strangers had brought treasures beyond price as gifts

for Jesus, piling them in a glittering heap beside the carpenter's bench. As she crept down little by little to look at the gifts more closely the spider grew more and more ashamed, and more and more sad that she was the only one who had still given nothing.

By the next night the strangers had gone again, back to their own countries, and suddenly the family seemed in a terrible state of anxiety. Hurriedly they packed a few of their belongings onto the donkey – including the gift the little spider had been sitting on. At dawn the donkey moved off and the spider went too – once more a stowaway.

They travelled south all that day and at dusk they found shelter in a cave on the mountainside. It was a damp cave and there wasn't much in the way of comfort – no hay, no fire.

'Why don't they light a fire?' wondered the spider. 'It would keep the jackals away, especially when the yard dogs aren't here to protect them either.'

She ran up and down the sides of the donkey's carrying bag, worrying and worrying, but keeping carefully out of sight in case she frightened Mary or the little boy.

Gradually Mary and Joseph fell asleep. Jesus patted the donkey's soft fur for a while then he slept too, sucking his thumb. The donkey sighed softly, easing his tired legs one after the other, dozing peacefully.

'Now I'm the only one awake,' thought the spider. 'I must be the one to keep watch.' So she crept out of the carrying bag and scurried across to the mouth of the cave. All night long she stayed there, running up and down the walls of the cave, swinging from side to side of the entrance, trying to be sure that she would miss nothing that might bring harm to the infant king.

At last, just before dawn, she heard the tramp of feet – soldiers' feet, soldiers with swords coming towards them. It was

Herod's men searching for the baby they must kill!

'Wake up, oh wake up!' she shouted as loudly as she could. 'You must wake up and leave as fast as you can! You'll be caught. Oh, please wake up!'

But a spider's voice is very small and everyone was sound asleep. The soldiers came up to the cave entrance.

'Too late, they're here,' the spider sobbed. 'I tried, I did try.'

Strangely, though, the soldiers didn't burst in. They stood outside.

'No one's in there, sir,' said the one at the front. 'Look at this wonderful spider's web right across the entrance. Whoever hid in there would have broken it as they escaped, but it's still perfect.'

And it was perfect – a glorious net of silk right across the cave mouth!

The soldiers went away and the family woke. Jesus looked at the web glistening with dewdrops in the first rays of the sun, and he laughed with delight and stretched out his hands to it. His mother picked him up and took him closer.

'Look,' she said to Joseph, 'there's a little spider here. And what a beautiful present she gave us – a crystal door to our cave to keep us safe.'

It was the best moment of the little spider's whole life! Mary was not frightened of her, and even better than that, she too had given a gift – the only gift she had to give – the gift of love.

**Isla Plumtree wrote this retelling of the
legend of the spider's web**

Isla lives in a hillside cottage overlooking the sea and surrounded by fields, forest, and sheep who peer in at the Christmas tree in winter.

Prayer idea:

Dear God, you loved people so much that you sent your Son, Jesus, into the world so that we could be friends with you. Help us to love you and worship you this Christmas. Amen.

'After the wise men had gone, an angel from the Lord appeared to Joseph in a dream and said, "Get up! Hurry and take the child and his mother to Egypt! Stay there until I tell you to return, because Herod is looking for the child and wants to kill him."' Matthew 2:13

The Camel Boy

(Reading time: 15 minutes)

The Camel Boy looked carefully around to check that no one was watching him. Then he lay down on the stony ground and rolled quietly under the dark canvas into his master's tent. His heart was thumping against his ribs. He had to be very careful not to be caught. His father had been caught. He had been a slave in the king's household and was found taking food to feed his hungry children. His father had been dragged before the angry king, who ordered that he be killed. The Camel Boy had run away from home that same day and hidden amongst some camels. It was there that his master had found him.

They had been travelling for two years, ever since that day, but he had never been inside his master's tent before. It was rich and magnificent. He listened carefully for any sound of voices near the tent and then stood up. The reason why he was taking this terrible risk was to find out why his master was travelling to Jerusalem. No one would tell him when he asked, and now they were camped outside the ancient city and it was his last chance to find out.

All he needed to do was to look inside the small wooden treasure box that his master always carried on his own camel. The tent was not big and he found the box easily. The answer was inside; but the box was locked.

The Camel Boy could hear voices approaching the tent.

He quickly lay back down against the canvas, ready to roll out into the sunshine again. The voices passed. He reminded himself to be careful and then began to search for the key. He picked up the heavy curved sword which he strapped to his master's camel every morning. He looked inside the soft leather travel bag which he tied round the animal's neck. Every time he picked something up, he replaced it in exactly the same position. Every time he put something down, he stood still for a while and listened. Eventually he found the key. It was tied, by a cord, to the inside of his master's cloak.

The Camel Boy unfolded the cloak and carried it over to the wooden box, keeping the key attached to its cord. He turned it in the lock. The box opened. Excitedly, but carefully, the Camel Boy unwrapped a layer of bright red silk. Underneath the silk, the box was packed with tufts of sheep's wool. These he counted into the box's lid, so he could be sure not to leave any lying on the ground. Tuft by carefully counted tuft, the boy uncovered a small golden crown. He lifted it out of the box. On the front of the crown was a bright, silver star.

'It's beautiful, isn't it?' a deep voice said close behind him.

It was his master. Absorbed in his counting, the Camel Boy had stopped listening to the sounds outside the tent. The boy turned round to face the tall, bearded man; the crown was still held in his sweaty hands. He said nothing. In his panic, all he could think of was himself, chained to the oar of a great slave ship, slowly dying under the painful lash of a slave-driver's long whip.

'Do you like it?' His master's voice was sweet, with no hint of anger. 'It is a gift for a child, a child who has been born a king.'

The Camel Boy was too afraid to speak. If he was afraid of his master, he was even more afraid of kings.

'If you would like,' his master continued, 'you may carry the crown for me today when we visit this child king. It may please him to see another child.'

The Camel Boy said nothing. He simply turned round, placed the small crown back in its place, quickly piled the wool on top, and closed the lid. He did not wait to lock the box, or to fold up the cloak. His master was standing in the entrance to the tent so the boy had to squeeze past him to get out. As he did so, he expected to be kicked or hit.

'I... I'm very sorry, sir,' he said weakly. 'I... I...'

'You need a wash, boy,' his master interrupted. 'And you will need clean clothes if you are to meet a king this afternoon.'

Then the boy ran quickly away and the man laughed.

Later on, the Camel Boy was dressed in new, white linen clothes, as the camel train set off on the last, short journey to Jerusalem. This time he was not at the back with the pack-camels where he usually rode. He rode with the masters on a camel of his own, holding the small treasure box which contained the star-adorned crown. The other masters were amused at the sight of the young slave boy, dressed up as though he were his master's own son.

'We do not know how old this child-king is,' his master explained to them. 'He may be frightened at the sight of us old men. Anyway, my Camel Boy is a Jew. It is his king we are visiting.'

The Camel Boy did not know what his master meant by calling him a Jew. His father had told him the same thing, but he never understood its meaning. Somehow, to hear that this child was his king made him even more frightened. You didn't have to be so afraid of someone else's king, but your own king... your own king would have power over you.

'His king.' The words echoed in his mind as he rode the short distance into Jerusalem and through the narrow streets to the Royal Palace. The more he thought about it, the more frightened he became. Kings were dangerous people and he did not want to meet one.

What if his master told this king how the Camel Boy had crept into his tent and been found helping himself to the crown? The king could have him killed!

At the Palace gate, the Camel Boy refused to go inside.

'I must look after the camels,' he insisted.

'The camels will be cared for by the king's servants,' his master told him.

'But I know these camels,' the boy said. 'I know what they need.'

'Wouldn't you like to meet your king?' his master asked.

'No! I'm not going in there,' the boy announced stubbornly.

'There is no need to be afraid,' his master assured him. 'It will be a memorable experience for you.'

The boy clung to the neck of his favourite camel and began to cry.

'Leave him,' one of the other masters urged. 'He's not worth it.'

The Camel Boy's master picked up the treasure box and disappeared into the Palace. The masters were inside for many hours and the boy was glad that he was there to care for his beloved camels.

The sun set and stars began to peep through the dark curtain of the night sky. He loved the stars. They were his friends at night as he lay among the camels. They were the same every night, no matter how far he travelled. He was comforted by the thought that somewhere, perhaps, his mother may be looking at the same stars and wondering what became of her son.

Something caught his eye. Low in the eastern sky, the Camel Boy spotted a star which he had not seen before. At the same moment, the masters emerged from the Palace.

'Boy!' his master called. 'Get the camels ready. We must travel again tonight.'

The boy was still staring at the new star when his master

walked up behind him and asked, 'What are you looking at?'

'There's a new star,' he replied, 'just above the horizon. Can you see it?'

'You are a clever boy,' his master exclaimed, ruffling his hair delightedly. 'That star is why we are here, and I believe that it is shining right above the town of Bethlehem. Quick, get to work. I want to follow it.'

As fast as he could, the Camel Boy had the camels kneeling in a row and he watched as the masters climbed aboard. In their hurry, they had forgotten how he had ridden with them that morning. He was now wearing a dirty old coat over his new clothes and was left to ride in his usual place, on the camel at the back of the train.

It did not take long to get to Bethlehem.

'Do you know where we are going?' asked one of the other masters.

'I am following that star,' the Camel Boy's master replied. He turned down a small alleyway and the others followed. At the end of the alley, in front of an ordinary-looking house, the road ended. The masters sat on their camels, wondering what to do next. The camel train completely filled the tiny street.

'Boy!' his master's voice called. 'Come here.' The Camel Boy slid down to the ground and scampered to the front camel. 'Good boy,' his master said. 'Go into that house and see if he is in there.'

The boy stood still for a moment, unsure who he was supposed to be looking for. 'Go on, get on with it,' said the impatient voice of one of the other masters.

The Camel Boy turned and ran in through the plain doorway into the lamp-lit single room of the house. The room was not unlike the simple home where he had lived with his mother and father before he ran away. Seated in the corner, he found a peasant girl who was nursing a young child. She looked up and smiled at the scruffy slave boy.

'Excuse me, Miss,' he said, 'I'm looking for the child-king, the King of the Jews.'

She seemed surprised, and then looked at her own child. 'He's right here,' she said. 'Would you like to come closer and see him?'

The Camel Boy pulled off his leather cap and knelt down beside the woman. He gently touched the infant's smooth forehead.

'You have a good eye for treasures, my boy,' his master's voice said from across the room. He was standing in the doorway, opening his treasure box. He took out the small golden crown and handed it to the Camel Boy.

'Here,' he said, 'would you like to give him this?'

Robert Harrison

Robert is the author of Oriel's Diary, *where the diary of Archangel Oriel records the birth, life, death and resurrection of Jesus Christ. Based on Luke's Gospel, it's an entirely original view of a familiar story. (Also available, two more books about Oriel:* Oriel's Travels *and* Oriel in the Desert.*)*

'A child has been born for us. We have been given a son who will be our ruler. His names will be Wonderful Adviser and Mighty God, Eternal Father and Prince of Peace. His power will never end; peace will last for ever. He will rule David's kingdom and make it grow strong. He will always rule with honesty and justice.' Isaiah 9:6,7

More great books for Christmas from Scripture Union...

Christmas Wrapped Up!

At last – the ultimate Christmas resource book! It really does contain practically everything a church might need for Christmas time. Includes service outlines, yuletide evangelism, plays, quiz questions, songs, craft, parties and games.

ISBN 1 85999 795 3

An Alien for Christmas

Brian Ogden

One particular Christmas turns out to be very different for Sophie – the Christmas she gets an alien by accident! Noughty is a funny and friendly visitor from planet Spam. Find out what happens when he secretly goes to school with Sophie, causes chaos at her church club, and gets off to a very bad start with her cat!

Suitable for 6- to 8-year-olds

ISBN 1 85999 595 0

Also available: two more books about Noughty and Sophie.

Noughty and the Alien SpamKam

Noughty the alien visits his friend Sophie again, this time bringing his latest invention with him – a SpamKam!

ISBN 1 85999 761 9

An Alien at Easter

Noughty's last visit from Planet Spam comes at Easter-time, and he's intrigued to find out all about hot cross buns, Easter eggs and Easter gardens.

ISBN 1 85999 760 0

The Angel Tree Adventure

Anne Thorne

Matt is not sure whether he will like being in America.

"Hamburgers are great and the ice cream is wonderful. It's just that I'm not used to facing Unidentified Fried Objects for breakfast!"

Then he meets Kim and Luke who show him an Angel Tree and they all decide to get involved. But none of them expects it to turn into an adventure or to end up being on TV! An exciting tale of intrigue revolving around the Angel Tree Project, which gives Christmas presents to the children of those in prison.

Suitable for 8- to 10-year-olds

ISBN 1 85999 474 1

Seasiders: Angels

Kathy Lee

It's Christmas, and the residents of Westhaven are puzzled by the disappearance of valuable paintings from the museum. But Grace's friends and neighbours have worries of their own. As she tries to go 'the extra mile' for those around her, Grace discovers that being kind can be costly.

And what will happen if it gets dangerous?

Will there be an angel around to help?

Suitable for 10- to 11-year-olds

ISBN 1 85999 523 3

You can buy all of these books at Christian bookshops, online at www.scriptureunion.org.uk/publishing or call Mail Order direct: 08450 706 006